Published by Creative Education
and Creative Paperbacks
P.O. Box 227, Mankato, Minnesota 56002
Creative Education and Creative Paperbacks
are imprints of The Creative Company
www.thecreativecompany.us

Design by The Design Lab
Production by Joe Kahnke
Art direction by Rita Marshall
Printed in the United States of America

Photographs by Alamy (Kevin Schafer), Corbis (W.
Perry Conway, Michael Durham/Visuals Unlimited,
HOLGER HOLLEMAN/epa, Radius Images, Duncan
Usher/Minden Pictures), Dreamstime (Lukas Blazek,
David Burke, Isselee, Tatiana Morozova), Flickr (Fer-
nando Flores), iStockphoto (forestc, FRANKHILDE-
BRAND), SuperStock (Doug Plummer)

Library of Congress Cataloging-in-Publication Data
Riggs, Kate.
Raccoons / Kate Riggs.
p. cm. — (Amazing animals)
Summary: A basic exploration of the appearance, be-
havior, and habitat of raccoons, the ring-tailed North
American mammals. Also included is a story from
folklore explaining why raccoons have masked faces.
Includes bibliographical references and index.
ISBN 978-1-60818-757-7 (hardcover)
ISBN 978-1-62832-365-8 (pbk)
ISBN 978-1-56660-799-5 (eBook)
1. Raccoons—Juvenile literature.
QL737.C26 2017
599.76—dc23   2016004915

CCSS: RI.1.1, 2, 4, 5, 6, 7; RI.2.2, 5, 6, 7, 10;
RI.3.1, 5, 7, 8; RF.1.1, 3, 4; RF.2.3, 4

First Edition HC 9 8 7 6 5 4 3 2 1
First Edition PBK 9 8 7 6 5 4 3 2 1

AMAZING ANIMALS

RACCOONS

BY KATE RIGGS

CREATIVE EDUCATION • CREATIVE PAPERBACKS

The common raccoon is a North American animal. Its masked face is seen in backyards and fields. It lives in the woods and in cities.

A hole in a tree makes a good den for a raccoon

There are two other kinds of raccoon. The pygmy raccoon lives on Cozumel Island in Mexico. Crab-eating raccoons are found in Central and South America. All raccoons have black fur around their eyes. They have rings of different-colored fur on their fluffy tails.

*A pygmy raccoon
(left); a crab-eating
raccoon (above)*

Raccoons can be many different sizes. Most common raccoons weigh about 8 to 20 pounds (3.6–9.1 kg). In winter, raccoons lose a little weight. They can squeeze through tight spaces.

A raccoon can fit into any space big enough for its head

Scraps of human food in a trash can make an easy meal

Raccoons are **native** to the Americas. They like living near trees and water. Many people see raccoons near their homes at night. Raccoons in cities and parks learn to look for food in trash.

native coming from a certain place

Raccoons eat whatever they can find. Their front paws are like hands. They can open containers. They can feel through mud. Raccoons scratch and clean food before they eat it.

Lidded boxes, latches, and doorknobs are no match for a raccoon

*Kits stay in a den
high above the ground
for several weeks*

A female raccoon has two to five **kits**. The kits are born with a face mask. But the rest of their fur is lighter colored. They hide in a den. The kits learn how to find food. Their mother teaches them to stay away from **predators**.

kits baby raccoons

predators animals that kill and eat other animals

Bobcats, coyotes, and other animals hunt young raccoons. Cars can be dangerous to raccoons, too. Raccoons run quickly to get away. They can run up to 15 miles (24.1 km) per hour.

A raccoon's whiskers stick out when it is scared or curious

Most raccoons live three to four years in the wild. They have areas called home ranges. Sometimes female raccoons and their young live together. Up to four male raccoons may share a home range.

Female raccoons choose ranges closer to their mothers than males do

Raccoons look for food wherever they go. Keep your trash cans closed. These nighttime animals are good at solving problems!

A raccoon can remember how to solve a problem for three years

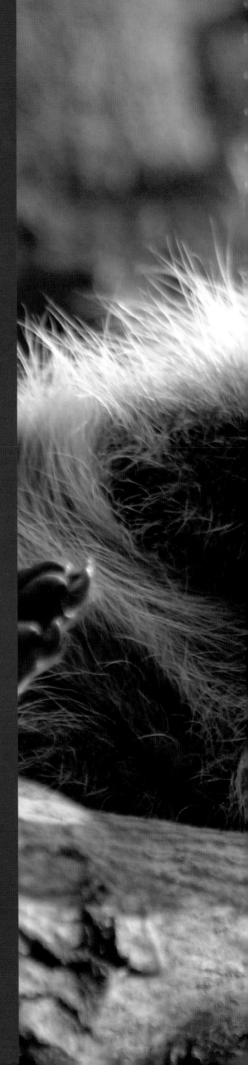

A Raccoon Story

Why does Raccoon wear a mask? American Indians of the Great Plains told a story about this. Long ago, Raccoon played a trick on Crayfish. He lay so still that Crayfish thought he was dead. Raccoon fell asleep after lying there so long. When he awoke, he was in a pit with a fire above him! He rubbed his eyes with his sooty paws and has had a mask on his face ever since.

Read More

Green, Emily. *Raccoons*. Minneapolis: Bellwether Media, 2011.

Johnson, Jinny. *Raccoon*. Minneapolis: Smart Apple Media, 2014.

Websites

Enchanted Learning: Raccoon
http://www.enchantedlearning.com/subjects/mammals/raccoon
/Raccoonprintout.shtml
Learn more about raccoons and print out a picture to color.

National Geographic Kids: Raccoon
http://kids.nationalgeographic.com/animals/raccoon/#raccoon-grass.jpg
This site has raccoon facts and videos of these clever animals in action.

Note: Every effort has been made to ensure that the websites listed above are suitable for children, that they have educational value, and that they contain no inappropriate material. However, because of the nature of the Internet, it is impossible to guarantee that these sites will remain active indefinitely or that their contents will not be altered.

Index